A Ticket to

India

Tom Streissguth

Carolrhoda Books, Inc. / Minneapolis

Photo Acknowledgments

Photos, maps, and artworks are used courtesy of: John Erste, pp. 1, 2−3, 8−9, 23, 39, 42−43; Laura Westlund, pp. 4−5, 27; © Air India Library, pp. 6, 36 (bottom); © Trip/H. Rogers, pp. 7, 9, 17 (top), 18 (bottom), 20, 23, 29; © Jean S. Buldain, pp. 8−9, 12 (bottom), 25 (bottom); © Courtesy of Embassy of Pakistan, p. 10; © Trip/Dinodia, pp. 11, 14, 15, 19, 24, 43 (bottom); © Trip/T. Bognar, p. 12 (top); © John Elk, pp. 12 (middle), 21; © American Lutheran Church, pp. 16, 34; © Brian Vikander, pp. 17 (bottom), 44; © Trip/Resource Foto, pp. 18 (top), 30; © Gerald Cubitt, p. 22; ©Trip/B. Turner, p. 25 (top); © Agence France Presse/Corbis-Bettmann, p. 26; © Courtesy of Minneapolis Public Library and Information Center, p. 27; © Don Eastman, p. 28; © Michelle Burgess, pp. 31, 32 (both); © Trip/B. Vikander, p. 33; © Tony Tigwell, p. 35; © TG Malhotra/Visuals Unlimited, p. 36 (top); © Trip/P. Rauter, p. 37; © Dinodia Picture Agency/Ravi Shekhar, pp. 38, 41; © Trip/W. Jacobs, p. 39; © Beverly Arenz, p. 40; © Trip/C. Wormald, p. 42; © Trip/B. Gibbs, p. 43 (top); © Dinodia Picture Agency, p. 45. Cover photo of kids © Jean S. Buldain.

Carolrhoda Books, Inc.
c/o The Lerner Publishing Group
241 First Avenue North
Minneapolis, Minnesota 55401 U.S.A.

Website address: www.lernerbooks.com

Library of Congress Cataloging-in-Publication Data

Streissguth, Thomas, 1958−
  India / by Tom Streissguth
    p.   cm.—(A Ticket to)
  Includes index.
  Summary: Discusses the people, geography, religion, language, customs, lifestyle, and culture of India.
    ISBN 1−57505−136−2 (lib. bdg. : alk. paper)
    1. India—Juvenile literature. [1. India.] I. Title II. Series: Ticket to (series)
DS407.S86 1999
954—dc21   98−15235

Manufactured in the United States of America
1 2 3 4 5 6 − JR − 04 03 02 01 00 99

Contents

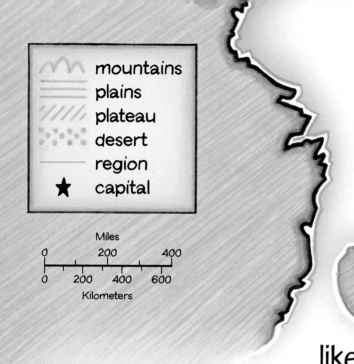

〜〜	mountains
≡≡≡	plains
⁄⁄⁄⁄	plateau
∶∶∶∶	desert
——	region
★	capital

Miles

0   200   400

0   200   400   600

Kilometers

India takes up a lot of space on the **continent** of Asia. On a **map** of the world, India looks like a diamond. Pakistan, China, Nepal, Bhutan, and Bangladesh touch India's northern side. And see the land east of Bangladesh and west of Myanmar (once called Burma)? That region is called Assam and is part of India, too. The Bay of Bengal, part of the Indian Ocean, is east of India. The Arabian Sea lies to the west. Off the southern tip of India sits Sri Lanka, an island country shaped like a teardrop.

Making Mountains

How do mountains form? Think of the continents as chunks of ice floating on a pond. What happens when two pieces smash into one another? They might bounce off one another. Or one piece may slide on top of the other piece. A long, long time ago, India was not part of Asia. When India crashed into Asia and stuck, mountains called the Himalayas joined the two. The Himalayas are the highest mountains in the world.

(Above left) *Mountaintops in the Himalayas get lots of snow.* (Left) *Have you ever taken a ride on a camel? They are still one of the best ways to cross the Desert of Thar in northwestern India.*

Big River

Rowing a boat can be hard work. These guys make it look easy as they glide on the Ganges River.

Splash! Many rivers flow through India. But the most important river is the Ganges. Get this: it is 1,500 miles long! It starts in the Himalayas and chugs across the **plains** of northern India. Eventually, the Ganges empties into the Bay of Bengal.

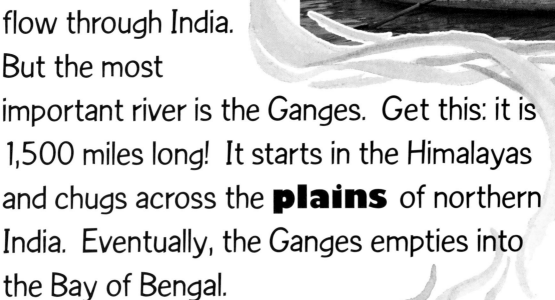

Map Whiz Quiz

Take a look at the map on page four. Trace the outline of India onto a piece of paper. See the Bay of Bengal? Mark this side of your map with an "E" for east. Find the Arabian Sea. Put a "W" for west here. With a green crayon, color in India. Color Nepal, Bhutan, and Bangladesh yellow to show where they end and India begins.

Don't forget to scrub behind the ears! Many Indians start their day with a bath in the holy Ganges. Not only does the water wash their bodies, it cleanses their spirits, too.

First Indians

What a place for a treasure hunt! About 70 years ago, scientists found this old city called Mohenjo-Daro. The town was buried under layers of dirt along the Indus River, a river that runs through India and Pakistan.

Long ago a group called the Dravidians built many towns in northern India. They lived in brick homes and farmed for a living. They knew how to count and how to write.

Many years later, the Aryans swept into the same area. They pushed the Dravidians

Adivasi

The oldest of all Indian groups are the Adivasi, who lived in India long before the Dravidians or the Aryans did. The Dravidians and the Aryans pushed the Adivasi into remote places, where they still live. The Adivasi follow their own customs.

into southern India. The Aryans spoke and wrote in an ancient language called Sanskrit.

Smile! These folks from Orissa still dress in the traditional clothes worn by their ancestors, the Adivasi.

Mixing Cultures

Two boys from Madurai in the southern state of Tamil Nadu pose for a picture.

(Above) *Women from the state of Rajasthan in northwestern India shop at the market.*

A brother and sister in the northern state of Kashmir

These days Dravidians and Aryans make up the two major **ethnic groups** in India. The members of each group have the same language and religion. Descendants of the Dravidians still live in the south. They are the largest group in India. Groups with ties to the Aryans live in the north. India has many smaller ethnic groups, too. The Tamils speak Tamil. They live in the southern state of Tamil Nadu.

Meeting and Greeting in India

Indians generally don't shake hands. When meeting someone, they bring the palms together in front of the chest, with the fingers pointing upward. They say *"namaste,"* which means "I bow to thee," and make a slight bow.

This sign is in Brahmi script.

Language

Most people in India speak English or Hindi.
But there are also 16 other major languages.

Many developed from old languages brought by Aryans.

The majority of Indians in the north speak Hindi. The government hopes to make Hindi the national language. But in the south, many people refuse to speak Hindi. They are worried that if everyone uses Hindi, the local languages will die out.

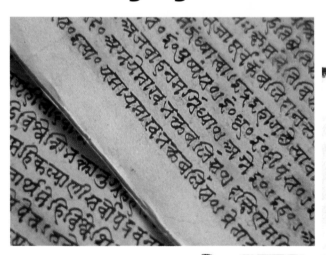

Alphabet Soup

The Hindi alphabet has 46 different letters—33 consonants and 13 vowels. Each letter stands for a certain sound. In this alphabet, the letters in a word are linked with a line across the top. Hindi is related to the ancient language called Sanskrit, shown here.

Getting Around

Beep, beep! Cars, buses, and people squeeze through a crowded intersection in an Indian city.

How does your family get around? Most Indians use bicycles, motorbikes, taxis, or their feet. Not many families own a car. When Indians have a long way to travel, they take a train or a bus. Chickens, dogs, cats, and even goats climb on board for the trip. Trains are sometimes so packed that passengers have to ride on the roof!

People pile on top of a crowded bus in Calcutta, India. Hang on tight!

Ganesh

Why does this crazy elephant have a human body? Because he is Ganesh, the god of wealth and wisdom. Hindus, people who practice the religion of Hinduism, believe that he also protects travelers. Roadside shrines to Ganesh can be found around the country.

Religions

(Right) *A Buddhist monk prays at a temple (holy place) in Sarnath.*
(Below) *A Hindu woman in Calcutta blesses the water by sprinkling flowers into the Ganges River.*

People practice many different religions in India. These include Islam, Sikhism, and Jainism. But most Indians follow Hinduism.

Many Indians learn about religion when they are very young. Children listen to stories from the *Ramayana* or the *Mahabharata*, two long, ancient Hindu tales.

Hindu Gods

There are many Hindu gods. Each has his or her own job. Brahma, Shiva, and Vishnu are the three most important gods. Brahma creates. Shiva destroys. Vishnu maintains order.

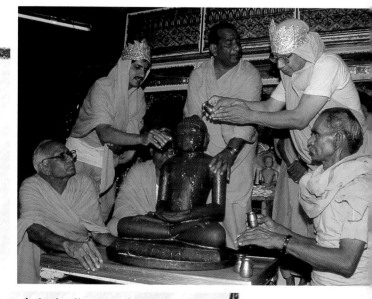

Jain believers bathe one of their gods at the Bath of Mahavira in Rajasthan.

Many untouchables, members of the lowest caste, live together in small villages like this one.

Caste System

All Hindus and Jains belong to a **caste,** or specific social group. In India, people are born into their caste, which has strict rules. People from different castes cannot eat together, for example. The caste system is against the law, but most people still follow it.

Castes and Jobs

There are four groups in the caste system. Each has its own set of jobs. Brahmans are priests and teachers. Kshatriyas are soldiers, rulers, and administrators. Vaisyas are merchants and craftspeople. Sudras are farmers and laborers.

This sadu, or Hindu traveler, comes from the highest caste of Brahmans. Sadus give up everything to spend time searching for religious truth.

Village Life

Do you live in the city or in the country? Most of India's people live in villages. Their houses are made of clay, brick, or even palm leaves. Traditional homes have an open **courtyard** in the middle. The family eats, works, reads, and talks in the

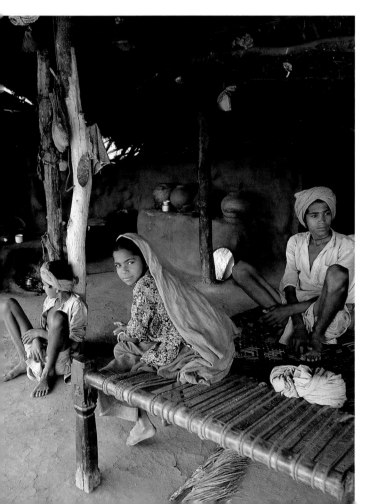

Take a peek inside this country home in Rajasthan. The girl and boy are sitting on charpoys, wooden beds made of rope netting.

A mom and her little boy take in some sun in their family courtyard. Can you see his older sister hiding in the shadows?

courtyard. When it is hot, the whole family sleeps in the courtyard. Just like one big family slumber party!

Shoes Outside!

In the countryside or the city, neat rows of shoes and sandals sit outside Indian homes. In India shoes are thought to be unclean because they touch dirty streets all day. Everyone takes off his or her footwear before they enter a home. In the house, people walk barefoot.

23

Lots of People

Imagine that all of your extended family members live in your house. When your parents have a party, each family member invites 160 friends. Jam-packed, right?

Rows of houses built from cardboard and scrap metal provide shelter for the homeless of Mumbai.

Calcutta, a city in northeastern India, is very crowded. So many people in one city cause big problems.

(Left) *Homeless people live on some Calcutta streets.*
(Below) *People shop in a crowded market in New Delhi's old city.*

Sometimes there is not enough water to go around. Thousands of people sleep in the streets because they do not have a home.

Two Indias

New Delhi is full of modern and ancient structures. Satellite dishes share the skyline with the Jama Masjid temple.

In India the old and the new are side by side. Temples built hundreds of years ago dot the countryside. But India also has computers, freeways, and high-rise buildings.

Many Indians live in both worlds. At home they follow old religious ways.

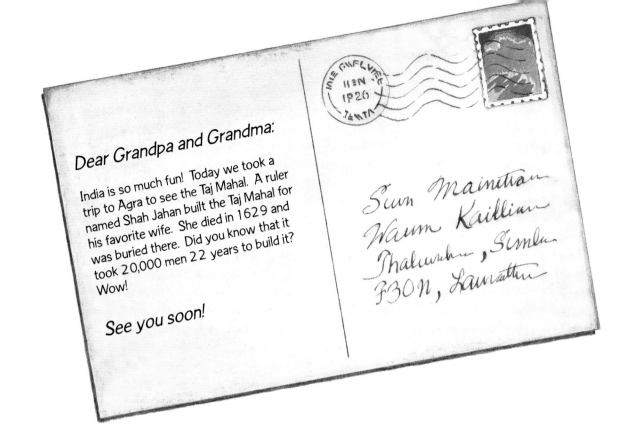

Dear Grandpa and Grandma:

India is so much fun! Today we took a trip to Agra to see the Taj Mahal. A ruler named Shah Jahan built the Taj Mahal for his favorite wife. She died in 1629 and was buried there. Did you know that it took 20,000 men 22 years to build it? Wow!

See you soon!

At work they communicate with cell telephones and personal computers.

The Taj Mahal, on the banks of the Yamuna River, is made of white marble.

Everyone in this busy farm family took time out for a picture in front of their home.

Family

Whom do you live with? Indian kids usually share a home with a few brothers and sisters, their parents, and their grandparents. Sometimes even aunts, uncles, and cousins are part of the household.

All in the Family

Here are some Hindi words for family members.

grandfather	*dada*	(dah-DAH)
grandmother	*dadi*	(dah-DEEH)
father	*pita*	(pi-TAAH)
mother	*mata*	(mah-TAAH)
uncle	*chacha*	(CHAH-chah)
aunt	*chachi*	(CHAH-cheeh)
son	*beta*	(bae-TAH)
daughter	*beti*	(BAE-teeh)
brother	*bahai*	(BHAA-ee)
sister	*bahan*	(BE-ha-nh)

A Hindu bride and groom in Calcutta wear traditional wedding clothes during the ceremony. Indian marriages are thought to join two families, not just two people.

29

Yum! Looks good enough to eat. But be careful! Indian food can be very spicy. Be sure to drink milk if your tongue starts to burn.

Food

Time to eat! Everybody gathers around a low table and takes a seat on a cushion. Most Indians eat with their fingers. They roll meat, vegetables, and **curry,** a spicy sauce, into a flatbread called **chapati.**

What happens if you get food on your fingers? Go ahead and lick them. In India it is okay to chew loudly, to pick your teeth, or to burp during the meal.

Women and men make chapatis at a community kitchen in New Delhi.

Sacred Cows

Killing a cow in India is strictly against the law. In the old days, cows were an important source of milk and butter. They kept people from starving, so Indians did not kill them. These days cows roam the streets and nobody bothers them. In the city of Varanasi, there is even a nursing home for aging cows.

Clothing

To keep cool, Indians wear light, loose clothing. Men and boys usually put on a collarless white

(Above) *These men wear dhotis, a light cloth that is wrapped around the waist and between the legs.* (Left) *Some Indians take their dirty clothes to a laundromat, called a dhobi. These dhobi workers on the banks of the Ganges have separated clothes by color and clothing type.*

cotton shirt over light
cotton pants.

Indian women and
girls wrap themselves in
a long, narrow piece of
cloth called a *sari*. They
wind saris around their
bodies in different ways,
depending on the day
and where they live.

*This little girl looks happy to
be wearing a brightly
colored sari. Fancy silk
saris come with a gold
border, called a palu. The
bigger the palu, the more
expensive the sari.*

In Indian schools, kids may sit on the floor or at desks. Sometimes classes are even held outside!

School Days

Kids in India start school when they are six years old. Boys and girls usually do not share the same classroom. In fact, girls from small villages often do not go to school at all. They stay home to help their mothers.

The school day lasts from eight o'clock until noon. Kids study math, Indian history, and geography. Most students also study English and Hindi or their local language.

Ten-year-old Sakina is learning to write in Hindi. She uses her black wooden slate to practice.

Holidays

Once a year, the people of India celebrate Children's Day. Parents hold small parties for their kids.

One of the most important Hindu festivals is Holi.

(Above) *Gotcha! During Holi people throw colored powder at their friends.* (Left) *Folks have fun with sparklers during Diwali, the festival of lights.*

It marks the coming of spring. Diwali, the Hindu festival of lights, takes place in the fall. Families clean their homes, light oil lamps, trade candy, and set off fireworks.

These women float candles on a lake to celebrate Diwali.

The wide-open spaces on a beach make it a great place for a game of cricket. Try not to hit the ball into the water!

Cricket Time

Indians love cricket. And we are not talking about a bug! Cricket is a little like baseball—but *only* a little.

Two teams of 11 players play a cricket match. One team bats while the other team fields. Players hit the ball and run between two bases called wickets to score points. If the batter hits the ball and a fielder catches it, then the batter is out. After 10 outs, the teams switch places.

Professional cricket players wear protective pads on their arms and legs.

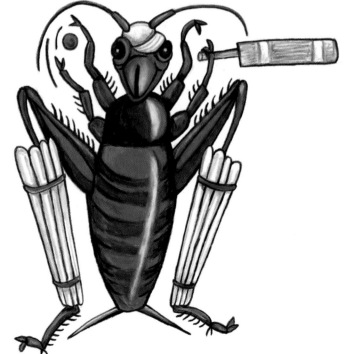

The Raj Mandir movie theater in Jaipur looks pretty empty, but just wait until the weekend. It will be packed!

Movies

India makes more movies than any other country in the world—sometimes as many as 800 films in one year! Each Indian film follows a certain plot. All movies have action, romance, and comedy. Like Hollywood pictures, good guys fight bad

Wondering what movie to see? Just look around you. In Indian cities, advertisements for the latest Hindi movies can be found all over town.

guys, and the good guys always win in the end. But in Indian films, the actors sing and dance to show what is going on.

Music

Two stringed instruments, the sitar and the *tanpoura*, make Indian music sound different from the music you are probably used to hearing. A drummer beats a rhythm on two small drums. The tanpoura player strums a

Some musicians, like this one in Rajasthan, sit on street corners and play songs for money.

single note, over and over again. The sitar player plucks notes in time to the rhythm. The sitar sounds a bit like a long, high-pitched cry.

(Above) The straps on these drums make it easy for the drummers to pound on the go. (Right) Do you like to dance? In India dancers move their hands, neck, and eyes in special ways to tell a story.

43

New Words to Learn

Elephants were once a good way to get around India. These days they carry tourists or guard royal palaces like this one in Jaipur.

caste: A social group that holds a traditional place and occupation in Hindu or Jain culture.

chapati: A flatbread, made from whole wheat flour and cooked on a griddle, that is eaten throughout India.

continent: Any one of seven large areas of land. The continents are Africa, Antarctica, Asia, Australia, Europe, North America, and South America.

courtyard: An open area, similar to a yard.

curry: A mixture of spices used to flavor meat or vegetables.

ethnic group: A large community of people that shares a number of social features in common such as language, religion, or customs.

map: A drawing or chart of all or part of the earth or sky.

plain: A broad, flat area of land that has few trees or other outstanding natural features.

One kind of Indian art goes right on your body. It is called mehndi, the art of body painting. People get mehndi designs like these for weddings or other special events.

New Words to Say

Adivasi	AH-dee-vah-see
Brahman	BRAH-mee-nh
chapati	chah-PAH-tee
Diwali	dee-WAH-lee
dhoti	DH-oo-tee
Ganges	GAH-n-gah or GAN-jeez
Himalayas	himh-ah-LAYH-az
Hindi	HIHN-dee
Hinduism	HIHN-doo-iz-em
Jainism	JEYE-niz-em
kshatriya	kesh-at-REE-ah
Mahabharata	mah-HAH-bha-rah-tah
mehndi	MEH-an-dee
namaste	nah-mah-STAY
Punjabi	pun-jah-BHEE
Ramayana	RAH-mah-ya-naah
Sikhism	SEE-kh-iz-em
Sri Lanka	SREE lahng-kuh
Taj Mahal	TAAJ mah-hawl
Tamil Nadu	TAH-mil nah-DOO
tanpoura	than-POO-rah

More Books to Read

Das, Produpta. *I Is for India.* Parsippany, NJ: Silver Press, 1997.

Dasgupta, Dagmar. *An Indian Home: Tulu's Story.* New York: Homestead Press, 1988.

Ganeri, Anita, and Rachel Wright. *India: Country Topics for Craft Projects.* New York: Franklin Watts, Inc. 1994.

Haskins, Jim. *Count Your Way through India.* Minneapolis: Carolrhoda Books, Inc., 1990.

Hermes, Jules. *The Children of India.* Minneapolis: Carolrhoda Books, Inc., 1993.

Madavan, Vijay. *Cooking the Indian Way.* Minneapolis: Lerner Publications Company, 1985.

Quigley, Lillian. *The Blind Men and the Elephant: An Old Tale from the Land of India.* New York: Scribners, 1959.

Schmidt, Jeremy. *In the Village of the Elephants.* New York: Walker and Company, 1994.

Stuart, Jane. *I Am Indian American.* New York: Powerkid Press, 1997.

Tigwell, Tony. *A Family in India.* Minneapolis: Lerner Publications Company, 1985.

New Words to Find